Chapter One Workbook

Meredith Bond

Published by Anessa Books, Alexandria, VA

Table of Contents

Introduction

Welcome to the Chapter One Workbook!

You *don't* have to have read my book on writing, ***Chapter One: A Fun, Fast Way to Write Fiction*** in order to use this workbook. This book is for every writer who wants a little help organizing their writing.

Nowadays there are so many different ways of organizing your writing, of getting started with a novel, or of analyzing it once it's written, depending on whether you're a "plotter" or a "pantser". I happen to like the old-school method of filling in worksheets—sometimes on the computer, sometimes printed out.

For every work of fiction I write (and as of this month, January 2018, I've published 17 works including three novellas, a short story and the rest being full-length novels), I create a notebook – both a virtual one using Microsoft OneNote and a physical notebook. My virtual notebook I mainly use for my research, as it's a great place to keep snippets from websites and pictures. My physical notebook is filled with these worksheets—some filled in, some left blank to be filled in as I write.

I start my plotting with worksheets, I use them throughout the entire writing process, and then when I've finished my book, I go back through them in order to write my book description. I find them an indispensable tool in my writer's toolbox.

And now I'm going to give them all to you.

I've tried to make them as useful as possible, creating fillable PDFs (you can find them at http://meredithbond.com/ihtt8PplcTBt4) as well as blank worksheets in this book that you can copy and use. If you have any problems with the links I mention in this book, please email me and I will do my best to make sure they work properly and you get your worksheets.

As a writer, you understand the importance of not sharing copyrighted material, and so I will ask you to please not share these worksheets or the links in this book with anyone. If they want one worksheet, have them write to me and I will share freely. If they want more than that, please ask them to purchase their own copy of this book.

Each worksheet is accompanied by a short description, although most are self-explanatory. If you need more explanation than what I give here, please check out my book ***Chapter One,*** where you'll find detailed explanations of each different aspect of writing.

If you'd like to suggest changes to any, feel free to email me. As a professional writer, I am always reading, learning and changing the way I do things. The ones here are what I think are the most useful at this time. I hope you'll find them useful as well.

Thank you, and happy writing!

Merry

Getting Started

When you first come up with an idea for a book, it's important to get as much of that idea down as quickly as possible. This worksheet allows for that. It's here for you to summarize your idea, your characters and your plot quickly and easily. It's also the one I come back to first when I'm getting ready to write my book descriptions, because that too needs to be as concise as possible.

When Starting a Book Don't Forget:

What's the **kernel idea**? The spark?

Characters

Hero: ____
Internal GMC
He wants __________________________ because _______________________ but
_____________________________ therefore ________________________________.
External GMC
He wants __________________________ because _______________________ but
_____________________________ therefore ________________________________.

Unique characteristics of this person:

What is their wound? And how does it shape their life?

What's important to them?

How do they react to a crisis (run away, face it down, think it through)

What's the worst thing that can happen to this person?

Heroine: ____
Internal GMC
She wants _________________________ because _______________________ but
_____________________________ therefore ________________________________.
External GMC
She wants _________________________ because _______________________ but
_____________________________ therefore ________________________________.

Unique characteristics of this person:

What is their wound? And how does it shape their life?

What's important to them?

How do they react to a crisis (run away, face it down, think it through)

What's the worst thing that can happen to this person?

Antagonist: ____
Internal GMC
They want _________________________ because _______________________ but
_____________________________ therefore ________________________________.

External GMC

They want _______________________________ because _______________________________ but _______________________________ therefore _______________________________.

Unique characteristics of this person:

What is their wound? And how does it shape their life?

What's important to them?

How do they react to a crisis (run away, face it down, think it through)

What's the worst thing that can happen to this person?

What makes them lovable?

****

Primary Secondary Characters

Name: _______________________________ Relationship _______________________

Name: _______________________________ Relationship _______________________

Name: _______________________________ Relationship _______________________

Name: _______________________________ Relationship _______________________

Name: _______________________________ Relationship _______________________

****

What is the **story question**?

What's at **stake**?

Where's the sense of **urgency**?

****

Plot out the Narrative Structure

Inciting incident:

Major Turning Point:

Rising Action:

Crisis:

Climax (black moment):

Resolution:

Characters

I always start out my plotting with characters – you may have noticed that on the previous worksheet.

I start with a thorough examination of the goal, motivation and conflict that drives my protagonist, and therefore the story, and then move onto other details.

I've got four worksheets for you to use to examine your protagonist(s):

The first is the Character Examination Worksheet. I believe everything you'll find there is pretty straight forward. The only part that you might have questions about is the section on Personality Traits. These are an Adjective which can be used to describe your protagonist (just one word!), a Noun, an Irony (something unexpected about this person), and a Verb (what it is that the person is doing throughout the book).

For example, we might fill that section out in the way for Dorothy from the Wizard of Oz:

Adjective:	**Noun:**	**Irony:**	**Verb:**
Confused	Teenager	Brave	Searching

Dorothy is a confused teenager—she starts out seeking attention, then runs away from home, only to return as soon as she hears that her aunt is sick. She then spends the rest of the movie bravely searching for a way home through the land of Oz where she meets, and sometimes even befriends, all sorts of strange creatures, not to mention an evil witch. Obviously, the witch doesn't become a friend, but Dorothy does stand up to her—not the actions of a cowardly, scared teenager.

The last two rows of the table below that are for you to identify your protagonist's identity, potential, wound and belief. These are terms taken from the teachings of Michael Hauge. If you ever have an opportunity to take a seminar with him, do it! He gives amazing one and two day seminars. He also has a website where you can learn a lot and buy his books and videos: https://www.storymastery.com/.

To fully understand, and be able to fill out those boxes, skip forward to the following worksheet: Hauge's Internal Conflict Questions. On this worksheet, these four terms are explained.

I then have an alternative Character Worksheet that takes a slightly different take on how you might want to get to know your characters better. And for the third worksheet, I provide the opportunity for you to take a thorough, long look at your characters to see what sort of person they might be.

And finally, I've got a worksheet for you that is just a simple way to keep track of your secondary (and tertiary, if you'd like) characters.

Character Examination Worksheet

Physical Traits

Name: ____ Age:______

Hair color, texture, length:

Eye color, size, shape:

Body type:

Distinguishing marks or scars:

How to do they speak that is particular to them?

Favorite words, sayings, phrases, exclamations:

Personality Traits

Adjective:	Noun:	Irony:	Verb:

Character Traits

Internal Goal	Internal Motivation	Internal Conflict
External Goal	External Motivation	External Conflict
Strength	Worst Fear	Deep Secret
Identity	Potential	Values (3)
Wound	Belief	Vulnerability

Michael Hauge
Internal Conflict Questions:

What is the hero's **<u>longing</u>**? What do they say they want, but don't actually go after because they're too afraid to do so?

What is the hero's **<u>wound</u>**?

What is the hero's **<u>belief</u>**? Out of the wound they believe the world works in a certain way. What is that way?

What is the hero's **<u>fear</u>**?

What is the hero's **<u>identity</u>**? Their outside persona, the one they show to the world?

What is the hero's **<u>essence</u>**? Strip away the identity and what is left? What does he have the **<u>potential</u>** to become?

Main Character

Name: ____ Age: ______

Brief Physical Description:

Where was s/he born?:

What family does s/he have and how does s/he feel about them?

What does s/he want when the story begins?

Why?

What has s/he done so far towards getting this?

What does s/he plan to do next?

What is the worst thing that could happen to mess up this goal?

Write down an adjective and a noun to describe her/him (example: Dorothy is a confused teenager, Hans Solo is a cocky smuggler).

Long Character Worksheet

Name:
Age:

Physical Description
Hair:
Body build:
Eyes:
Distinguishing features:

Where did s/he grow up?
City?
Suburbs?

List 4 things about the character's childhood that affect who s/he is today:

Is s/he type A or B?

Did s/he grow up rich or poor?

How many siblings does s/he have?

Who has died in her/his immediate family and how did it affect her/him?

What's the best thing that happened to her/him in his/her childhood?

Worst thing?

Was s/he loved by her/his parents?

Was s/he the favorite child? Second favorite? Least favorite?

Do s/he collect certain objects?

What is her/his favorite thing?

What sorts of things do s/he keep around her/him?

What do you, as author think her/his best quality is?

What is her/his worst quality?

What does s/he think is her/his best quality?

Worst quality?

What does s/he dislike (personality traits in others)? Is it because s/he shares that trait?

Is the character hiding anything from the world or themselves?

What does s/he want? Does s/he know this?

What is her/his favorite curse?

What is her/his favorite expression?

What endearments does s/he use the most and to whom?

Does s/he have a distinctive rhythm of speech?

What is her/his greatest fear?

What's the last thing s/he would want to give up and what would drive her/him to give this up?

Secondary Characters

Name:____ Age:_____

Physical Description: ____

Relationship to hero/heroine: _________________________________

Goal: ____

****

Name:____ Age:_____

Physical Description: ____

Relationship to hero/heroine: _________________________________

Goal: ____

****

Name:____ Age:_____

Physical Description: ____

Relationship to hero/heroine: _________________________________

Goal: ____

****

Name:____ Age:_____

Physical Description: ____

Relationship to hero/heroine: _________________________________

Goal: ____

****

Name:____ Age:_____

Physical Description: ____

Relationship to hero/heroine: _________________________________

Goal: ____

Story Structure

There are a lot of ways to outline your story structure. Some people swear by Blake Snyder's Save The Cat, others prefer a more basic outline, some prefer the tried and true Hero's Journey.

I have to admit, Save the Cat never resonated with me, but don't worry, I've got plenty of different story structure worksheets one of which is bound to fit your book.

I start out with the most basic story structure: the 'W' graph. This is the only worksheet that doesn't have an associated fillable PDF, because you need to be able to place your text wherever you want along the line. We then move to two different types of outlines; the Hero's Journey (a worksheet I created based on Christopher Vogler's **The Writer's Journey**); and then back to Michael Hauge with a worksheet based on his six stage story structure.

Once again, if you need a more detailed description of these different structures, you'll find it in **Chapter One**.

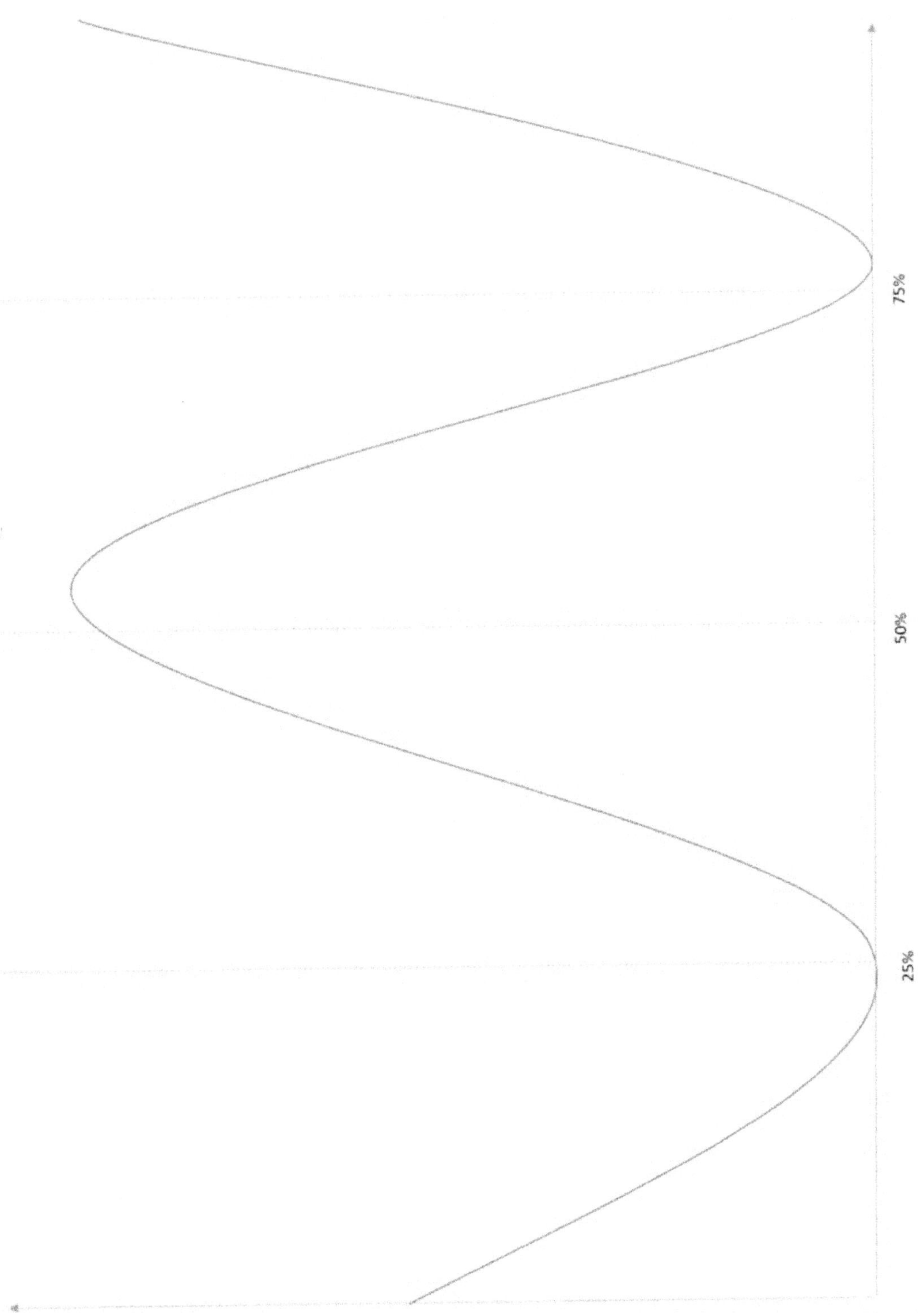
75%
50%
25%

Story Outline

Act I

Inciting Event:

Stimulus:

Response:

Decision:

New Situation/Major Turning Point:

Stimulus:

Response:

Decision:

Act II

Progress:

Stimulus:

Response:

Decision:

Midpoint/Point of no return/Climax:

Stimulus:

Response:

Decision:

Complications and higher stakes:

Stimulus:

Response:

Decision:

Act III

Black Moment/Crisis:

Stimulus:

Response:

Decision:

Resolution:

Stimulus:

Response:

Decision:

Story Outline

Act I

Inciting Event:

Goal:

Conflict:

New Situation/Major Turning Point:

Goal:

Conflict:

Act II

Progress:

Goal:

Conflict:

Midpoint/Point of no return/Climax:

Goal:

Conflict:

Complications and higher stakes:

Goal:

Conflict:

Act III

Black Moment/Crisis:

Goal:

Conflict:

Resolution:

Goal:

Conflict:

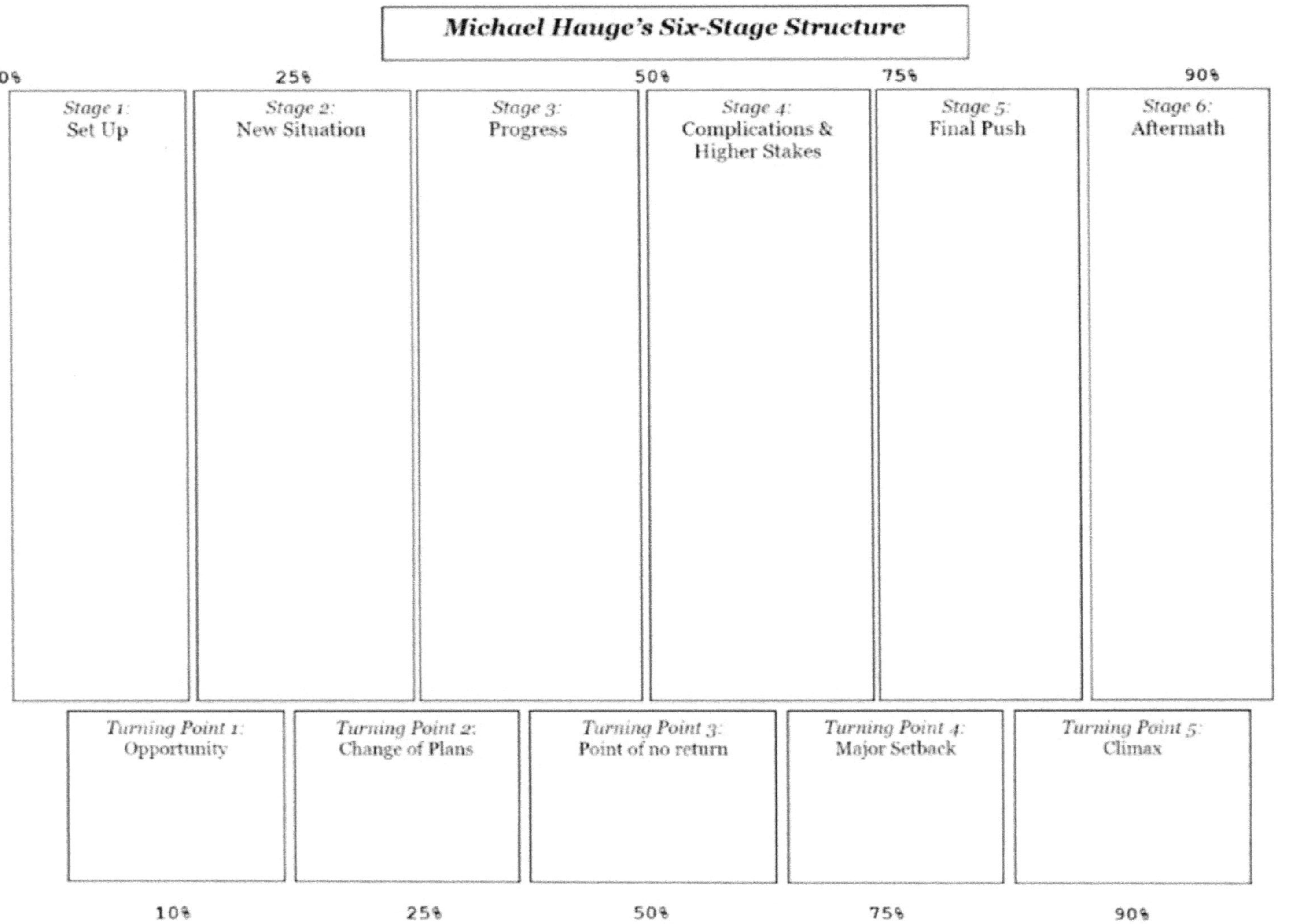
Michael Hauge's Six-Stage Structure
0%
25%
50%
75%
90%
Stage 1: Set Up
Stage 2: New Situation
Stage 3: Progress
Stage 4: Complications & Higher Stakes
Stage 5: Final Push
Stage 6: Aftermath
Turning Point 1: Opportunity
Turning Point 2: Change of Plans
Turning Point 3: Point of no return
Turning Point 4: Major Setback
Turning Point 5: Climax
10%
25%
50%
75%
90%

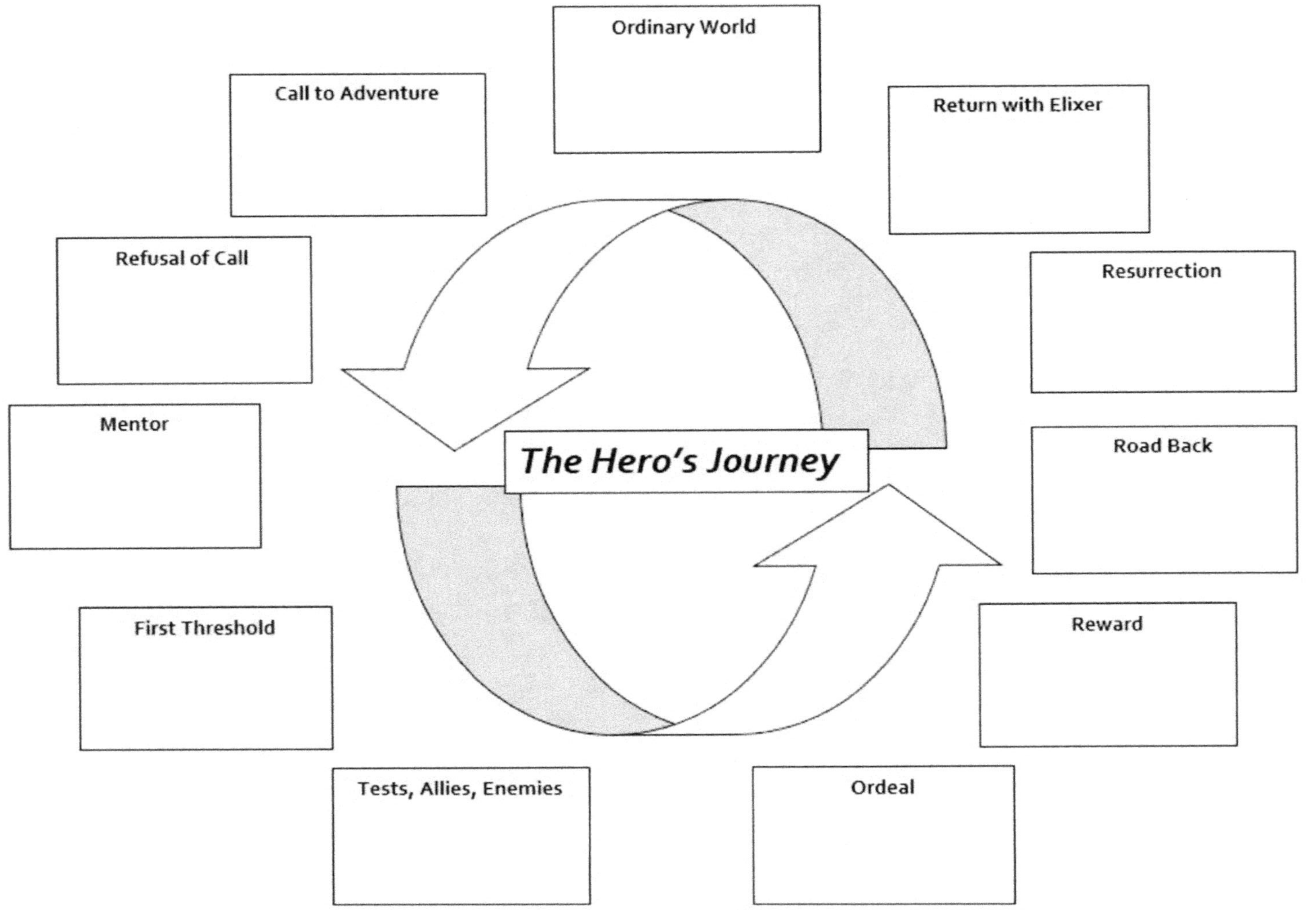
Ordinary World
Call to Adventure
Return with Elixer
Refusal of Call
Resurrection
Mentor
The Hero's Journey
Road Back
First Threshold
Reward
Tests, Allies, Enemies
Ordeal

Scenes

We now move on to the building blocks of our novel—the scenes. I've got three worksheets for you. The first is a basic scene outline; I've then got an alternative way of breaking down your scene; and finally, a general table for you to keep track of your scenes. A word about each one:

The scene outline worksheet is straight forward, and I'm sure you won't have any questions about it. However, I would like to point out that the second to last question, "Why does this matter...?", comes from my reading of Lisa Cron's wonderful book **Story Genius.** In it she talks about the protagonist's "Third Rail", which is basically what that question is asking about. If you have questions about this concept, I highly recommend reading **_Story Genius_**. Her first book, **Wired for Story**, is also a fascinating read. Both can be found on her website http://wiredforstory.com/.

For the second scene worksheet, everything is pretty straightforward. The section, "What needs to be fixed?" is meant to be filled out after the book is written and you're going through each scene in detail. The basic components of the scene, and, if necessary, the next one.

One note about the scene table: I've left the last three columns blank. Those are for you to fill in with things that you need to keep track of in your writing. For example, when I write, I always leave out the five senses. When I'm finished writing and beginning my editing process, I'll read through and make a note in this chart where I need to add in more of the five senses in my descriptions. You might also want to have a column for sexual tension or romance if you write romance, for magic if you write paranormal, etc. Whatever you need to keep track of as you edit your work, put that down here in this chart.

Scene Outline

Scene Title: ____Day# ___

Locale: ____

Time of day: ____

POV Character: ________________________________

Scene Summary:

What is the author's purpose for the scene?

1.

2.

3.

What is the high moment/disaster?

What is the inner conflict?

What is the outer conflict?

How does the POV character change or grow in the scene?

Why does this matter given the protagonist's internal goal and misbelief?:

Therefore (what happens next):

Scene Worksheet

Scene Title:	Place:
Character's Goal:	Problem/What happens?
Prize/Stakes:	
Strategy (attempts at scene goal) 1. 2. 3.	Opposition/Problem 1. 2. 3.
Initial Conflict to be resolved:	Turning Point/Disaster:
How does protag grow in scene?	Author's purpose of scene: 1. 2. 3.
How does antagonist grow in scene?	What do others in scene think about conflict?
What needs to be fixed? 1. 2. 3.	What is the story question in this scene?
	How does this scene set up next scene?

Quick Scene and Sequel Summary:

Scene	Sequel
Scene Goal:	Sequel Reaction:
Scene Obstacle:	Sequel Dilemma:
Scene Disaster:	Sequel Decision:

Scene #	POV	Brief description of what happens	Setting described	Conflict/Tension

Setting

And finally, I've got three worksheets for you on setting. The first is a general setting worksheet, the second is an exercise for you to run through when you really need to be deep within the POV character's head, and the third is a world building worksheet for writers of fantasy.

The first worksheet is completely straightforward. The second I got from Alicia Rasley. Like with Michael Hauge, if you ever have the opportunity to hear her speak, do not walk, but run to sign up. She is not only an amazing writer, she's a fantastic teacher of writing. Check out her website (http://www.aliciarasley.com/) too, she's got good craft articles there as well as a link to her fantastic book on Point of View. Her exercise is an adaptation of work by Les Edgerton.

Setting Worksheet

Story title:____

Year:____________

Country:____

City/town:____

How well does the Protagonist know this place?

How well does the Antagonist know it?

What does the Protagonist love about it?

Why do they hate it?

How does it make them feel?

What does s/he know about this place that no one else does?

What is their favorite place within the setting? Why?

What makes this place different from the reader's ordinary world?

POV Scene Grounding Exercise:

Where are you?

What do you see?

What is the time?

What is the light like?

What is your body doing?

What can you hear?

What does that sound mean?

What do you feel under your feet?

What do you feel in your hands?

What do you feel on your face?

What do you feel in your heart?

What can you smell?

What can you taste?

Who is with you?

What do you hope will happen?

What do you fear will happen?

Fantasy World Building

Story Title: ____

World Name: ____

What type of world is it: Modern, Medieval, Futuristic?

Physical World

Earth?

If not earth, what are the defining characteristics? (two suns, more than one moon, major mountain ranges, major bodies of water):

Society

How do people live: towns, villages, cities?

What sort of houses do they live in? Brick, wood, stone?

What is the level of technology? Modern, ancient, futuristic?

How to people get around? Cars, foot, horse, dragon?

What is medicine like? Doctors, priests, wizards, shaman?

What is the legal system?

How do people trade goods? Paper money, coins, barter?

What type of educational system is there? Public schools, private schools, private tutors, apprenticeships? Are there universities?

What is the system of government? Democratic, Feudal, Monarchy, Dictatorship?

What religion(s) are there? Do people go to temple, church?

Are there people of different races or is everyone the same? (and not just skin color, but elves, orcs, fairy, etc): Define each race, what it looks like and what special abilities they have.

Magic

Is there magic in the world?

More than one type?

How does it work?

Where does it come from?

Can it be transferred from one being to another or taken away?

What can be done?

What cannot be done using magic?

What is the price of using magic?

How do people feel about it?

Who can use magic?

Who cannot?

Conclusion

Thank you so much for working through all of these worksheets with me. I hope that you found something to make your writing and plotting easier. Remember, if you have any questions or want to see what else I have to offer, my website, www.meredithbond.com, is filled with useful blog posts and articles for writers. Explore and enjoy!

About the Author

Meredith Bond has been both traditionally and self-published. She has written over fifteen Regency romance and paranormal romance books and two works of non-fiction. She has been teaching writing and self-publishing since 2005 both in person and on-line and owns and runs her own formatting business, Anessa Books, where she not only makes the beautiful words of her clients look beautiful on page and screen, but guides new authors through the sometimes complicated process of self-publishing.

Her novels straddle that beautiful line between historical romance and fantasy. As an award-winning author, she writes fun traditional Regency romances, medieval Arthurian romances, and Regency romances with a touch of magic. Known for her characters "who slip readily into one's heart," Meredith loves to take her readers on a journey they won't soon forget.

You can learn more about Merry at her website, www.meredithbond.com, and more about her formatting work at www.anessabooks.com.

Website: www.meredithbond.com

Facebook: https://www.facebook.com/meredithbondauthor

Twitter: https://twitter.com/merrybond

Pinterest: http://www.pinterest.com/merrybond/

Goodreads: https://www.goodreads.com/author/show/847484.Meredith_Bond

Please don't forget to leave a review wherever you buy books.